THE

CHILD'S MONITOR;

OR

SELECT RULES FOR SPELLING THE

English Language:

with a few simple Questions in

ENGLISH GRAMMAR,

AND ARITHMETIC.

"Sorting, and puzzling with a deal of glee,
Those SEEDS of SCIENCE, call'd his A, B, C."
Cowper.

ROSS:

Printed and Sold by W. Farror ;

SOLD ALSO BY BALDWIN, CRADOCK & JOY, LONDON;
AND ALL OTHER BOOKSELLERS.

1824.

The Tutor's address to his Pupils.

—

My dear Boys,

In order that you may be well grounded in the Elements of your native tongue, it will be necessary that you should become thoroughly acquainted with the contents of this little Book.

With my sincere desire to promote your solid improvement,

I remain,

Your affectionate friend,

FIDELIS.

10th. May, 1824.

CHAPTER I.

OF THE LETTERS.

HOW many letters are there in the English Language?

Twenty-six.

What is a letter?

A letter is the first principle, or least part of a word.

Of what are the letters representatives?

They are representatives of certain articulate sounds, the elements of the language.

What is an articulate sound?

An articulate sound is the sound of the human voice, formed by the organs of speech.

How are letters divided?

Into vowels and consonants.

What are the vowels?

a, e, i o, u, and sometimes w and y.

What are the consonants?

b, c, d, f, g, h, j, k, l, m, n, p, q, r, s, t, v, w, x, y, z.

What is a diphthong?

A diphthong is the union of two vowels, pronounced by a single impulse of the voice; as, ea in beat, ou in sound.

CHAPTER II.

OF SYLLABLES.

What is a syllable?

A syllable is a sound, either simple or compound, pronounced by a single impulse of the voice, and constituting a word, or part of a word; as, a, an, ant.

What is spelling?

Spelling is the art of rightly dividing words into their syllables: or, of expressing a word by its proper letters.

What is a termination?

A termination is a letter or syllable that ends a word; sometimes called an ending.

SEVEN RULES

For the division of Syllables.

RULE I.

A single consonant between two vowels, must be joined to the latter syllable; as, de-light, bri-dal, re-source, ca-pa-ci-ty: except the letter x; as, ex-ist, ex-am-ine: and except likewise words compounded; as, up-on, un-e-ven, dis-ease.

The termination y is not to be placed alone: except in dew-y, snow-y, and a few others.

RULE II.

Two consonants proper to come together at the beginning of a word, must not be separated; as, fa-ble, sti-fle. But when they come between two vowels, and are such as cannot begin a word, they must be divided; as, *ut-most, un-der, in-sect, er-ror, cof-fin.*

RULE III.

When three consonants meet in the middle of a word, if they are proper to come together at the beginning of a word, and the preceding vowel be pronounced long, they are not to be separated; as, de-*thr*one, de-*stroy*. But when the vowel of the preceding syllable is pronounced short, one of the consonants always belongs to that syllable; as, di*s*-tract, di*s*-prove, di*s*-train.

RULE IV.

When three or four consonants, which are not proper to come together at the beginning

B

of a syllable, meet between two vowels, such of them as can begin a syllable, belong to the latter, the rest to the former syllable; as, ab-*stain*, com-*ple*te, em-*broil*, dan-*dler*, dap-*ple*, con-*strain*, hand-*some*, parch-*ment*.

RULE V.

Two vowels, not being a diphthong, must be divided into separate syllables; as, cru-*el*, de-ni-*al*, so-ci-e-ty.

RULE VI.

Two consonants which form but one sound, are never separated; as, e-*cho*, pro-*phet*, bi-*shop*.

RULE VII.

The terminations -*tion*, -*sion*, -*tial*, -*tious*, -*cious*, -*scious*, are to be spelled as one syllable; as, ac-*tion*, eva-*sion*, par-*tial*, cau-*tious*, pre-*cious*, con-*scious*.

CHAPTER III.

OF WORDS.

What are words?

Words are articulate sounds, used, by common consent, as signs of our ideas.

What are all words called?

All words are called either monosyllables, dissyllables, trisyllables, or polysyllables.

Define what you mean by these words respectively.

A word of one syllable, is termed a mono-syllable; a word of two syllables, is termed a dissyllable; a word of three syllables, is termed a trisyllable; a word of four sylla-bles or more, is termed a polysyllable.

What sort of words are participles?

They are words formed from verbs; as, to love, loving, loved; to say, saying, said; to travel, travelling, travelled.

How many participles are there?

Two.

Name them.

The active participle always ending in *ing*, and the passive participle invariably ending in *ed*, when formed from a regular verb.

How many terminations are there added to regular verbs, to form these participles?

Three.

Name them.

ing, *d,* and *ed.*

By what rules for spelling words, are you taught to spell all participles, thus formed from regular verbs?

By rules 3, 4, 5, 6 and 7.

What is accent?

Accent is a particular stress of the voice, laid on a certain syllable in a word; as, de-préss, cáncel, índustry.

What is meant by the singular number?

By the singular number is meant but *one* object; as, face, house, dog.

What is meant by the plural number?

By the plural number is meant *more objects* than *one*; as, faces, houses, dogs.

What do you mean by the word noun or substantive?

A noun or substantive is the name of an object, or of any thing of which we have any notion; as, face, house, dog, virtue, improvement.

THIRTEEN RULES,

for spelling words.

RULE I.

Monosyllables ending with *f*, *l*, or *s*, preceded by a single vowel, double the final consonant; as, staff, mill, pass.

EXCEPTIONS.

Of, if, as, is, has, gas, was, yes, his, us, and thus.

RULE II.

Monosyllables ending with any consonant but *f*, *l*, or *s*, and preceded by a single vowel, never double the final consonant; as, fib, mud, mug, sun, cur, nut.

EXCEPTIONS.

Add, ebb, butt, egg, odd, err, inn, bunn, purr, and buzz.

RULE III.

case 1st.

Words ending with *y*, preceded by a consonant, form the plural of nouns, the persons of verbs, verbal nouns, past participles, comparatives and superlatives, by changing *y* into *i*; as, spy, spies; I carry, thou carriest, he carrieth or carries, carrier, carried; happy, happier, happiest.

case 2nd.

The present or active participle in *ing* retains the *y*, that *i* may not be doubled; as, carry, carrying; bury, burying.

case 3rd.

Y preceded by a vowel in such instances as mentioned in case the 1st. is not changed; as, boy, boys, I cloy, he cloys, cloyed.

EXCEPTIONS.

Lay, laid, pay, paid,

Unlay, unlaid, unpay, unpaid.

Repay, repaid, stay, staid.

RULE IV.

case 1st.

Monosyllables, and words *accented* on the *last* syllable, ending with a *single* consonant, preceded by a *single* vowel, double that consonant when they take another syllable, beginning with a vowel; as, wit, wit*t*y; thin, thin*n*ish; to begin, a beginner, beginning; to abet, an abettor, abet*t*ing, abet*t*ed.

case 2nd.

If a *diphthong* precedes, or the *accent* is on the *preceding* syllable, the consonant remains single, when another syllable beginning with a vowel is added; as, to toil toiling, toiled; to offer, an offering, offering, offered; maid, maiden.

EXCEPTIONS.

Wool, woolly, woollen.

Quit, quitting, quitted.

Acquit, acquitting, acquitted.

Equip, equipping, equipped.

Ferret, ferretting, ferretted.

Fillet, filletting, filletted.

Rivet, rivetting, rivetted.

Wherret, wherretting, wherretted.

Worship, worshipping, worshipped.

RULE V.

Words ending in *il*, *al*, or *el*, with no other vowel in the syllable, having terminations added to them beginning with a vowel, double the *l*, whether the last syllable is accented, or not accented; as, cavil, cavil*l*er, cavil*l*ing, cavil*l*ed; equal, equal*l*er, equal*l*ing, equal*l*ed; cancel, cancel*l*er, cancel*l*ing, cancel*l*ed.

RULE VI.

When *ing*, or *ish* is added to words ending with silent *e*, the *e* is almost universally omitted; as, place, placing; lodge, lodging; slave, slavish; prude, prudish; blue, bluish; white, whitish.

*** For spelling words in *ing*, which might be placed as EXCEPTIONS to this rule, see Rule vii.

RULE VII.

Words ending with *double* consonants, with *two* vowels, or with *two* consonants, retain those letters when the terminations *ness, less, ly, ful, ing, d* or *ed,* are added; as, harmlessness, carelessly, successful, illness, shrillness, stillness, smallness; to wax, waxing, waxed; to woo, wooing, wooed; shoe, shoeing, shoed; hoe, hoeing, hoed; flee, fleeing, see, seeing; fee, feeing, feed; agree, agreeing, agreed; disagree, disagreeing, disagreed; flow, flowing, flowed; form, forming, formed; indict, indicting, indicted.

EXCEPTIONS.

Words ending with double *l*, generally omit one *l*; as, full, fulness; skill, skilless; dull, dully, dulness.

Verbs ending in *ie*, change *ie*, into *y* before *ing*; as, die, dying; lie, lying; tie, tying.

All verbs ending in *ue*, drop the final *e*, when *ing* is added; and so do the verbs owe, awe, dye, eye, lye; as pursuing, owing, &c.

GENERAL RULE.

If a regular verb active ends in *e*, with a consonant preceding, *d* only is added to form the participle passive; as, decide, decided; discharge, discharged.

GENERAL EXCEPTIONS.

Do and go with their compounds, make doing and going; be, being; echo, echoing, echoed; subpœnaing, subpœnaed.

N. B. For the formation of passive participles of irregular verbs, see Murray's large Grammar, page 111.

RULE VIII.

Words ending with *i* preceded by a *consonant*, upon assuming an additional syllable, beginning with a consonant, commonly change *y* into *i*; as, happy, happily, happiness. But when *y* is preceded by a *vowel* it is very rarely changed in the additional syllable; as, coy, coyly; boy, boyish, boyhood ; annoy, annoyer, annoyance ; joy, joyless, joyful.

RULE IX.

Ness, less, ly and *ful*, added to words ending with silent *e*, do not cut it off; as, paleness, guileless, closely, peaceful.

EXCEPTIONS.

Duly, truly, awful.

RULE X.

Ment added to words ending with silent *e*, generally preserves the *e* from elision; as, abatement, chastisement, incitement.

EXCEPTIONS.

Judgment, abridgment, acknowledgment.

Observe. Like other terminations, *ment* changes *y* into *i*, when preceded by a consonant ; as, accompany, accompaniment ; merry, merriment.

RULE XI.

Able and *ible*, when incorporated into words ending with silent *e*, almost always cut it off; as, blame, blamable; cure, curable; sense, sensible; but agree and disagree make agreeable, and disagreeable : also, if *c* or *g* soft comes before *e* in the original word, the *e* is then preserved in words compounded with able; as, change, changeable; peace, peaceable.

RULE XII.

Compound words are spelled in the same manner, as the simple words of which they are formed; as, household, horseman, forenoon, wherein, skylight, glasshouse, telltale, snowball, molehill.

EXCEPTIONS.

When the letters are superfluous in the simple words; as, handful, dunghil, withal; also, chilblain, foretel, wherever, candlemas, christmas, lammas, martinmas, michaelmas.

RULE XIII.

The plural number of nouns is generally formed by adding *s* to the singular; as, dove, dove*s*; face, face*s*; thought, thought*s*.

D

EXCEPTIONS.

When the substantive singular ends in *x*, *ch* soft, *sh*, *ss* or *s*, we add *es* in the plural; as, box, box*es*; church, church*es*; lash, lash*es*; kiss, kiss*es*; rebus, rebus*es*. If the singular ends in *ch* hard, the plural is formed by adding *s*; as, monarch, monarch*s*; distich, distich*s*.

Nouns ending in *o* form the plural by adding *es*; as, cargo, cargo*es*. Those nouns in which *i* precedes *o*, add *s* only; as, nuncio, nuncio*s*; folio, folio*s*.

Nouns ending in *f* or *fe*, are rendered plural by the change of those terminations into *ves*; as loaf, loa*ves*; wi*fe*, wi*ves*: except, grief, relief, reproof, and several others, which form the plural by the addition of *s*. Those which end in *ff*, have the regular plural; as, ruff, ruffs; except, staff, staves.

Nouns which have *y* in the singular, with no other vowel in the same syllable, change *y* into *ies* in the plural; as, beauty, beauties; fly, flies. But the *y* is not changed when there is another vowel in the syllable; as, key, keys; delay, delays.

Some nouns become plural by changing the *a* of the singular into *e*; as, man, men; woman, women; alderman, aldermen. The words ox and child form oxen and children: brother makes either brothers, or brethren. Sometimes the diphthong *oo* is changed into *ee* in the plural; as, foot, feet; goose, geese; tooth, teeth; louse and mouse, make lice, mice; penny makes pence, or pennies, when the coin is meant: die, dice, (for play;) die, dies, (for coining.)

For the plural of words from the Hebrew, Greek and Latin Languages, see Murray's large Grammar, page 52.

CHAPTER IV.

QUESTIONS IN ENGLISH GRAMMAR.

(See Murray's small Grammar, page 9.)

What is English Grammar ?

Into how many parts is English Grammar divided ?

Name them.

What does orthography teach ?

Of what does etymology treat ?

Of what does syntax treat ?

Of what does prosody consist?

What does the former teach?

What does the latter teach?

How many parts of speech are there?

Name them.

What is an article?

Name the articles.

What is the article *a*, or *an* called?

Why?

When does *a* become *an*?

What is the article *the* called?

Why?

What is a noun or substantive ?

How may a substantive be in general distinguished ?

What is an adjective ?

How may an adjective be known ?

What is a pronoun ?

Give an example and shew how the pronoun is used for the noun ?

What is a verb ?

How may a verb be generally distinguished ?

What is an adverb ?

How may an adverb be generally known ?

What are prepositions ?

How may a preposition be known?

What is a conjunction?

Give your examples and shew which are the conjunctions.

What is an interjection?

Name the interjection in your example.

CHAPTER V.

QUESTIONS IN ARITHMETIC.

(See Walkingame's Tutor's Assistant, page 1.)

What is Arithmetic?

How many principal or fundamental rules has it, upon which all its operations depend?

Name them.

What does numeration teach?

What does addition teach?

What does it shew?

What does subtraction teach?

What does it shew?

What does multiplication teach?

E

What does it compendiously perform ?

How many principal numbers belong to this rule ?

Name them.

What is the multiplicand ?

What is the multiplier ?

What is the product ?

What does division teach ?

How many numbers are there in division ?

Name the three real numbers.

What is the accidental number ?

Of what name or denomination is the accidental number ?

—⊶⊷⊷⊶—

Omission, after Rule VII, *page* 11.

FIVE OBSERVATIONS.

1. Compounded words must be traced into the simple words of which they are composed.

2. Grammatical, and other particular terminations are generally separated.

3. Double consonants are generally separated.

4. *C* and *g* soft are added to the last syllable.

5. A consonant, if single, is joined to the termination, when the preceding vowel is long.

EXAMPLES.

Ice-house, over-power, never-the-less.

Teach-eth, teach-ing, great-er.

Beg-gar, fat-ter, bid-ding.

Cot-ta-ges, pro-noun-cer, in-dul-ging.

Ba-ker, sa-ved, ho-ping.

ERRATA.

Page 22.   Read subpœna before subpœnaing.
Page 22.   Rule VIII, line 1st. for *i* read *y*.

FINIS.

Printed by W. Farror, Ross.

www.ingramcontent.com/pod-product-compliance
Lightning Source LLC
Chambersburg PA
CBHW081307040426
42452CB00014B/2680

9 781535 802710